YORKSHIRE
STEAM
1948-1967

PETER TUFFREY

GREAT NORTHERN

ACKNOWLEDGEMENTS

Thanks are due to the following people: Roger Arnold; David Burrill; Paul Chancellor; Ron Fisher; David Joy; John Law; Hugh Parkin, Richard Postill; Bill Reed; Gerald T. Robinson; Sue, Andrew and Rachel Warnes; Anthony Watson; Bill Wright.

Gratitude should also be expressed to my son Tristram for his general help and encouragement throughout the course of the project.

PHOTOGRAPHS

Every effort has been made to gain permission to use the photographs in this book. If you feel you have not been contacted please let me know: petertuffrey@rocketmail.com

INFORMATION

I have taken reasonable steps to verify the accuracy of the information in this book but it may contain errors or omissions. Any information that may be of assistance to rectify any problems will be gratefully received. Please contact me by email: petertuffrey@rocketmail.com − or in writing Peter Tuffrey, 8 Wrightson Avenue, Warmsworth, Doncaster, South Yorkshire, DN4 9QL.

Great Northern Books
PO Box 1380, Bradford, BD5 5FB
www.greatnorthernbooks.co.uk

Every effort has been made to acknowledge correctly and contact the copyright holders of material in this book. Great Northern Books Ltd apologises for any unintentional errors or omissions, which should be notified to the publisher.

ISBN: 978-1-912101-25-2

Design and layout: David Burrill

CIP Data
A catalogue for this book is available from the British Library

INTRODUCTION

When assembling photographs for *The Last Years of Yorkshire Steam*, which was published in 2016, I was quite spoiled for choice and in the event space restricted the number of images that could be included in the collection. The quality of the remainder ensured that a second volume would follow and here we take another look at the rundown of steam in the Yorkshire area.

A study of steam locomotives in 'God's Own County' is particularly interesting given the varied scenery in which the subjects could be captured: from the rolling countryside to coastlines to industrial heartlands. This also led to diversity in the motive power used in the area, ranging from express classes to mixed traffic and dedicated freight engines, which was also split between larger engines and smaller shunters.

Another factor is the number of companies contributing different designs. Several railways established themselves in Yorkshire, such as the Great Northern, Great Central (formerly the Manchester Sheffield & Lincolnshire), Hull & Barnsley, Lancashire & Yorkshire, Midland, London & North Western and North Eastern. Then at Grouping in 1923 these companies were split between the London Midland & Scottish Railway and London & North Eastern Railway, which in turn produced their own locomotives; the same is true of British Railways after Nationalisation.

These railway companies operated a number of important routes through Yorkshire. The GNR had had part of the East Coast Main Line, with major connections to this at Doncaster and York; the GCR arrived from Manchester over the difficult terrain of the Pennines to reach the coalfield, Sheffield and through to the East Coast ports; the H&BR collected products from the coalfield to transport to Hull for export. Another major connection to Manchester and the North West was made by the L&YR, whilst the MR ran northward to Leeds, later extended to Scotland, with the ex-North Midland Railway route from Derby and the Midlands, as well as London. The LNWR had a relatively short connection to Huddersfield and Leeds and the NER controlled East and North Yorkshire.

Alongside these major routes were many smaller lines and connections, many of which were not remunerative, that were often just built for territorial reasons. For example, the GNR built lines in the difficult terrain west of Bradford to serve businesses there but the costs were high and were perhaps never recouped. An interesting connection was made south of Barnsley whereby the GCR bypassed the town, running from Silkstone to Wombwell. Yet, this line, which was freight only, had three miles at 1 in 40 – the Worsbrough incline – that was extremely difficult for the heavy coal and freight trains, often requiring several locomotives to assist; two photographs in this collection show this practice in operation.

The LNER and LMSR consolidated and improved on the lines and facilities – stations, sheds, etc – they inherited from their forebears at the Grouping of 1923. A particular project seen amongst the pictures here is the Wath-Manchester or 'Woodhead' electrification scheme started by the LNER before the war and completed under BR in the early 1950s.

A similar situation was experienced at Nationalisation in 1948, although British Railways was to come up against a rapidly changing transport landscape due to the growth in popularity of the motor car. This ultimately led BR to favour a rapid change towards diesel traction in order to dramatically reduce costs.

The sad result of this decision was the demise of the steam locomotive, which was an inherently dirty, noisy and temperamental machine, but loved by many across the nation having produced numerous instances of cherished childhood memories. This author had a particularly vivid encounter with Gresley A4 Pacific no. 60028 *Walter K. Whigham* at Doncaster in the early 1960s as the locomotive thundered through the station with a named express.

The post-war period also saw cameras become more affordable, allowing a growing number of enthusiasts to record the soon to be lost steam age for posterity. This dedicated band captured many fine images at stations, locomotive depots, from the lineside, goods yards and collieries, which now give us a window into the past.

Many of these evocative images are included here in *Yorkshire Steam* as the collection highlights many places across the county. A number of the major cities and towns are documented, such as Leeds,

Sheffield, York, Hull, Doncaster, Harrogate, Goole, etc, as well as smaller places like Arthington, Dunford Bridge, Staithes, etc.

A wide variety of locomotives are seen at these places, including many of the major Stanier Classes – 'Jubilee', Class 5, 8F – and Gresley designs – A3, D49, V2 – alongside others: Thompson B1, Peppercorn A1/K1, Robinson O4, Raven B16, WD 'Austerity' and Ivatt 4MT. The engines can be seen working a variety of services, ranging from named expresses to secondary passenger and local trains to coal and freight. There are also several specials seen as these became popular as the rundown of steam accelerated and drew ever nearer.

A small band of enthusiasts also ventured to collieries and captured the variety of tank locomotives moving coal, which was the most recognisable product from Yorkshire at the time. Although all the collieries have disappeared, a number of the engines have been saved due to the fact that steam continued under the National Coal Board working the colliery sidings even after the end of locomotives on the main line.

Continued interest in steam also led to the establishment of several heritage railways in Yorkshire, as well as the National Railway Museum in York. Alongside *Yorkshire Steam*, they celebrate the glorious history of steam in 'God's Own County'.

Peter Tuffrey
Doncaster, April 2020

Above ARDSLEY

View north west from Station Lane, Ardsley (south of Leeds), as Thompson B1 Class 4-6-0 no. 61339 approaches with a Leeds to Doncaster stopping train on 22nd April 1961. This view is now dominated by the M62 motorway and the sidings and line to Bradford (left) have been lifted. Photograph by B.W.L. Brooksbank.

Below ARMTHORPE MARKHAM MAIN COLLIERY

Built by the Hunslet Engine Co. in the early 1950s, 0-6-0ST *Arthur* arrived new to Markham Main Colliery, Armthorpe, near Doncaster, and worked there until sold for scrap in mid-1976. Photograph by John Law.

ARMTHORPE

Robinson O4/6 Class 2-8-0 no. 63911 has a train of mineral wagons at Armthorpe, near Doncaster, on 26th February 1955. The engine was allocated to Frodingham at this time but had moved on to Barnsley shed by the end of the year. Photograph by Geoff Warnes.

Above ASKERN COLLIERY
Following 18 years at Rossington Colliery 0-6-0ST *Rossington Colliery No. 1* moved to Askern Colliery in June 1968. The engine is there looking unloved on 16th April 1974 and would be scrapped on site in early 1977. Photograph by Geoff Warnes.

Below ARTHINGTON
Raven B16 Class no. 61470 pilots a Gresley A3 Class Pacific (no. 6008?) at Arthington in early 1958, passing Arthington South signal box. Photograph courtesy *Yorkshire Post Newspapers*.

Above ARTHINGTON STATION

The stationmaster at Arthington poses on the platform before the last weekend of operation on 18th March 1965. Photograph courtesy *Yorkshire Post Newspapers*.

Above ARKSEY
Thompson B1 no. 61399 appears to have been working hard during the two months in service from new when captured at Arksey, north of Doncaster, on 25th June 1952. The engine has a Colchester to York service. Photograph courtesy *Yorkshire Post Newspapers*.

Below ARKSEY STATION
The Great Northern Railway opened Arksey station on 5th June 1848 as part of a project to connect with the Lancashire & Yorkshire Railway's line from Wakefield to Goole at Knottingley. Originally named Stockbridge, the station became Arksey in 1854 and was used until 5th August 1952 when closed; the station is seen here shortly before that date. Photograph by Geoffrey Oates.

Opposite ARTHINGTON

The Leeds & Thirsk Railway (later renamed the Leeds Northern Railway) built the first station at Arthington which opened to traffic in April 1849. With the completion of the Otley & Ilkley Joint line by the Midland Railway and North Eastern Railway in 1865, a new station was built at the southern point of the triangular junction created. Here, during February 1958, Gresley D49/2 Class 4-4-0 no. 62738 *The Zetland* is at the northern point of the junction with a train of empty coaching stock. Photograph courtesy *Yorkshire Post Newspapers*.

Opposite below BARNBY DUN

Originally conceived as a robust and simple locomotive for handling freight traffic of the Great Central Railway, J.G. Robinson's 8K Class (London & North Eastern Railway O4 Class) underwent several modifications over the years resulting in no less than eight subclasses. No. 63788 was part of three during 48 years in service. Starting life from the North British Locomotive Company in June 1918, the engine was built for the Railway Operating Division of the British Army and was not taken into LNER stock until 1927 when classified O4/3. In 1939 the locomotive was rebuilt with a diagram 15A boiler from Gresley's O2 Class becoming O4/5 and would receive a diagram 100A boiler from Thompson's B1 Class in 1957, along with a side-window cab, resulting in a reclassification to O4/8. No. 63788 has a Class J freight at Barnby Dun, north east of Doncaster, whilst still an O4/5 on 26th February 1955. Photograph by Geoff Warnes.

Opposite above BARNBURGH

A group of local enthusiasts pose with WD 'Austerity' no. 90631 at Barnburgh (on the Dearne Valley Railway) on 24th May 1952. Photograph by Geoff Warnes.

Opposite below BARNSLEY COURT HOUSE STATION

The North Midland Railway bypassed Barnsley to the east when opened in mid-1840; the nearest station was Cudworth. The successor Midland Railway built a branch from Cudworth to Barnsley in the late 1860s, reaching the MS&LR line from Penistone. Barnsley Court House station was built just south of this junction and saw the first trains arrive on 1st May 1870. By the late 1950s many services to Barnsley Court House had been discontinued and this caused the closure of the station in 1960. This scene was captured around the time of the announcement in early 1959. Photograph courtesy *Yorkshire Post Newspapers*.

Below BARNSLEY SHED

Located on the eastern side of Barnsley Exchange station, Barnsley shed was opened by the Manchester, Sheffield & Lincolnshire Railway in the mid-1840s and, although later rebuilt, was in use until 1960. Robinson C14 Class 4-4-2T no. 67447 is seen in the yard during the late 1950s. The locomotive was a resident there from November 1957 until early 1959 when condemned. Photograph by Bill Reed.

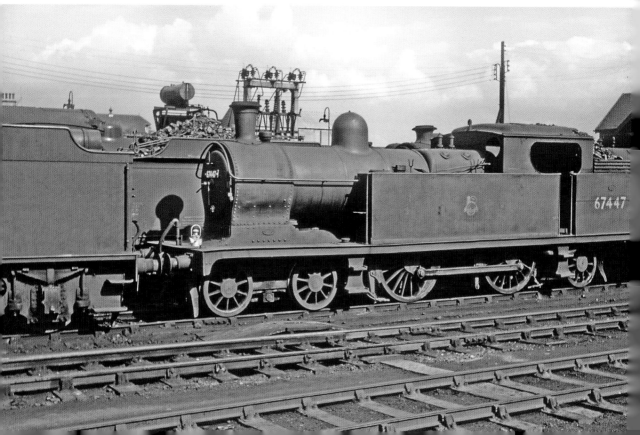

Above BARNSLEY COURT HOUSE STATION
Services from Cudworth to Barnsley Court House ended from 9th June 1958. Here on the 8th June, Johnson 1P Class 0-4-4T no. 58066 has been pictured between working the last trains. Photograph by Geoff Warnes

Below BARNOLDSWICK STATION
Fowler 4P Class 2-6-4T no. 42394 appears to be working hard to get away with the 08.19 service from Barnoldswick to Skipton on 1st August 1964. Photograph by Gerald T. Robinson.

Above BAWTRY STATION

War Department 'Austerity' Class 2-8-0 no. 90316 passes through Bawtry station, south of Doncaster, with a train of coal wagons on 5th December 1964. Photograph by Geoff Warnes.

Below BAWTRY STATION

Thompson B1 Class 4-6-0 no. 61275 of York shed takes the up main line through Bawtry station on 5th December 1964. Photograph by Geoff Warnes.

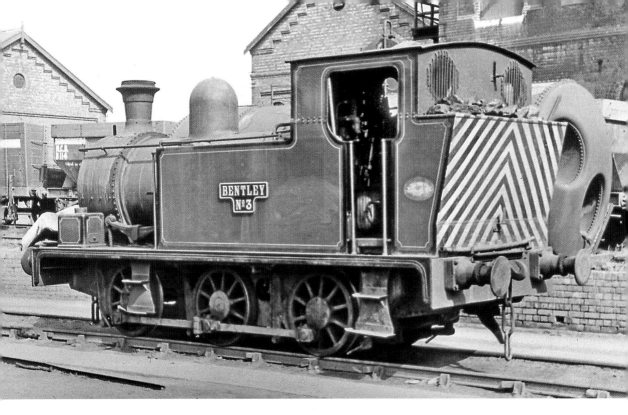

Above BENTLEY COLLIERY

Although this image appears to show one locomotive – *Bentley No. 3* – at Bentley Colliery in 1964, there are actually three masquerading as one. *Bentley No. 3* was built by Hudswell Clarke & Co. Ltd in 1909 and was at Bentley Colliery as *Bentley* for nationalisation of the industry in 1947. By the early 1960s, the engine was in need of overhaul and parts were cannibalised from *Bentley No. 2* (also erected by Hudswell Clarke & Co. Ltd in 1909) and *Bentley No. 3* (similarly built by the company in 1910) which returned the engine to traffic by mid-1963. *Bentley No. 3* continued to work on site until 1973. Photograph courtesy John Law.

Opposite above BEIGHTON

Robinson O4/3 Class 2-8-0 no. 63861 is at Beighton (south east of Sheffield) with a train of empty coal wagons on 25th September 1954. The locomotive was built by the NBLC in July 1919 and was not bought by the LNER until October 1927. First allocated to Immingham, the engine soon moved on to Tuxford and remained there until September 1953 when reallocated to Langwith Junction near Mansfield. No. 63861 was rebuilt to O4/8 specifications in November 1957 and was in this form until withdrawn in February 1965. Photograph by Geoff Warnes.

Opposite below BEIGHTON

View north alongside the ex-Midland Railway line at Beighton as WD 'Austerity' Class 2-8-0 no. 90649 approaches with loaded coal wagons from one of the many local collieries on 13th July 1963. The locomotive was built by the Vulcan Foundry in July 1944 and worked in Europe for a time before returning to England in 1947. After three years in storage, no. 90649 returned to service at Farnley Junction in February 1950 and was allocated there until July 1959 when moved to Huddersfield. In January 1967 a transfer to Normanton occurred but withdrawal took place soon after. Photograph by B.W.L. Brooksbank.

Above BEVERLEY ROAD STATION

In the second half of the 19th century, the citizens of Hull thought the North Eastern Railway shunned the city, especially the docks, in favour of others further up the coast. As a result the Hull, Barnsley & West Riding Junction Railway & Dock Co. (later just the Hull & Barnsley Railway) was formed to promote traffic from the coalfields to Hull. Beverley Road station in the city was one opened with the line on 27th July 1885. Following the formation of the LNER, the company diverted passenger traffic from the H&BR terminus at Cannon Street to Hull Paragon station and Beverley Road was closed in mid-1924; the remains are seen here on 20th May 1967. Photograph by B.W.L. Brooksbank.

Opposite above BEVERLEY STATION

View north from the platform at Beverley station as Ivatt Class 4MT no. 43076 heads a local freight service on 28th August 1963. Introduced in 1947, the Class 4 2-6-0s were built to replace older 0-6-0 locomotives at work for the London Midland & Scottish Railway. A total of 75 were constructed for the London Midland Region at Horwich Works between 1947 and 1952, whilst 87 were erected at Doncaster (50) and Darlington (37) for use elsewhere on the network. No. 43076 was completed at Darlington in October 1950 and was dispatched to Hull Dairycoates depot. The engine was still based there at the time of this picture and would have spells at Royston, Leeds Holbeck and Bradford Low Moor before condemned during September 1967. Photograph by Richard Postill.

Opposite below BEVERLEY STATION

The Hull & Selby Railway oversaw construction of the line from Hull to Bridlington via Beverley and Driffield. The line was ready for the first trains in early October 1846 and featured stations designed by noted architect G.T. Andrews. Beverley station is pictured on 18th April 1961 and has thankfully survived relatively unmolested by modern architects up to the present time. Photograph by B.W.L. Brooksbank.

Above BIRDWELL STATION

Robinson C13 Class 4-4-2T no. 67409 has a local service at Birdwell station during the early 1950s; the locomotive was withdrawn in December 1956. Photograph David Joy collection.

Below BRADFORD EXCHANGE STATION

On 10th October 1967 Fairburn 4P Class 2-6-4T no. 42141 is at Bradford Exchange station. Photograph by Geoff Warnes.

Above BRADFORD FORSTER SQUARE STATION

Stanier 'Jubilee' Class 4-6-0 no. 45593 *Kolhapur* arrives at Bradford Forster Square station on 30th April 1966 to take out the Jubilee Railway Society's service to Carlisle. The engine had to be replaced there by 'Britannia' Pacific no. 70035 *Rudyard Kipling* for the return journey. Photograph by Les Flint courtesy John Law.

Below BRADFORD

The 09.45 express to King's Cross heads away from Bradford Exchange station on 26th August 1967 with Fairburn 4P no. 42085 in charge. Photograph by Gerald T. Robinson.

Above **BRADFORD LOW MOOR SHED**
Charles Fairburn's 4P Class 2-6-4T design was the final development of the type introduced in 1927 by Sir Henry Fowler for medium-distance passenger services. Fairburn's locomotives were slightly lighter and had a shorter wheelbase than their forebears. A total of 277 were erected over five years from 1945, with the majority leaving Derby Works, although a number were built for the Southern Region at Brighton in the early 1950s. No. 42116 was completed at Derby in July 1949 and employed at Bradford Low Moor shed. The engine remained on the roster there until condemned in July 1967 and is in the shed yard earlier in the year on 19th February. Photograph by Geoff Warnes.

Opposite **BRADFORD LOW MOOR**
Thompson B1 no. 61306 approaches Low Moor, Bradford, with a train of empty coaching stock from Bradford Exchange on 27th July 1967. The locomotive entered service from the NBLC to Hull Dairycoates shed in April 1948 but transferred to Hull Botanic Gardens shortly after. No. 61306 remained there until June 1959 when returning to Dairycoates and would only move once more to Bradford Low Moor in June 1967. Withdrawn just three months later, the engine was subsequently preserved and found a home at Steamtown, Carnforth, where no. 61306 was given the name *Mayflower* from withdrawn classmate no. 61379. Recently undergoing a major overhaul, the engine is currently active on heritage services across the country. Photograph by Gerald T. Robinson.

BRADFORD LOW MOOR SHED

A few weeks after withdrawal, Fairburn 4P no. 42116 is at Bradford Low Moor shed. Photograph by Gerald T. Robinson.

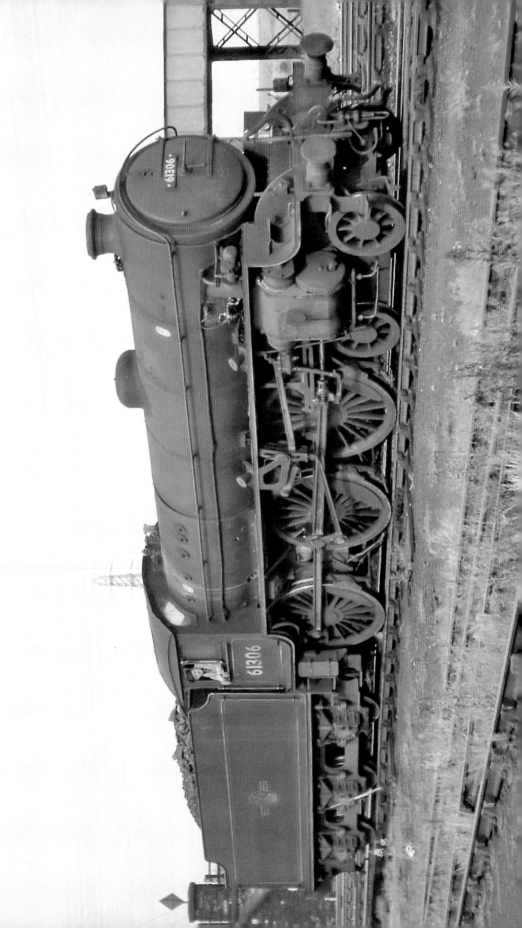

BRADFORD LOW MOOR
Thompson B1 no. 61306 is light engine at Bradford Low Moor on 27th July 1967. Photograph by Gerald T. Robinson.

Above BRADFORD LOW MOOR SHED
L&YR Aspinall Class 27 0-6-0 no. 52461 stands out of service at Bradford Low Moor Shed on 21st February 1960, with WD 2-8-0 no. 90711 also present. Photograph by Geoff Warnes.

Below BRADFORD LOW MOOR SHED
Stanier Class 5 4-6-0 no. 44694 arrived new at Bradford Low Moor in November 1950 and only spent two years away at Mirfield from mid-1964. Pictured on 19th February 1967, the engine was condemned in September. Photograph by Geoff Warnes.

Above BRADFORD LOW MOOR SHED
Withdrawn from Wakefield in June 1967, Thompson B1 no. 61388 waits at Bradford Low Moor to be dispatched to the scrapyard at the end of July. Photograph by Gerald T. Robinson.

Below BRADFORD LOW MOOR SHED
Stanier 4P Class no. 42587 is at the end of a line of locomotives waiting to be taken to the cutter's torch at Bradford Low Moor on 27th July 1967. Photograph by Gerald T. Robinson.

Above BRADFORD LOW MOOR

Stanier initially developed the Fowler 4P Class 2-6-4T to use three cylinders for work on the London, Tilbury & Southend Railway line. Yet, these engines soon proved to be little better than their predecessors and Stanier decided to perpetuate the original design only with slight alterations. A total of 206 were produced between 1935 and 1943. No. 42616, which is seen here at Bradford Low Moor on 22nd July 1967, was one of a large batch built by the NBLC in 1936 and 1937, being released to the LMSR in February 1937. In the BR era, the locomotive had a large number of allocations, although many of these occurred during the 1960s. No. 42616's residency at Low Moor depot occurred for just a brief spell from June to September 1967 when withdrawn. Photograph by Gerald T. Robinson.

Opposite BRADFORD LOW MOOR SHED

Whilst the Manchester & Leeds Railway bypassed Bradford by a distance to the south, the company and the successor Lancashire & Yorkshire Railway soon had plans in hand for connections to be made. By the early 1850s two of the company's lines converged at Low Moor: one from Halifax and another from Mirfield. The line then ran northward from Low Moor to Bradford Exchange station. The L&YR established a locomotive shed on the western side of Low Moor station in the mid-1860s and some 20 years later modernised the facilities. This consisted of the erection of a 12-road shed with coal stage combined with water tank; a mechanical coaler was later provided by the LMSR. Stanier Class 5 no. 44694 is reversing into the shed yard on 22nd July 1967; closure of the depot occurred in early October. Photograph by Gerald T. Robinson.

Above BRIDLINGTON STATION
A northbound passenger service waits at the platform of Bridlington station on 29th August 1964 with Stanier Class 5 no. 45133 at the head. Photograph by Richard Postill.

Opposite above BRADFORD FORSTER SQUARE
Stanier 'Jubilee' Class 4-6-0 no. 45697 *Achilles* has collected carriages from the sidings just north of Bradford Forster Square station on 5th August 1967. The Leeds Holbeck engine had just a month left in traffic and had been in service from April 1937. Photograph by Gerald T. Robinson.

Opposite below BRIDLINGTON SHED
Located on land just to the south west of Bridlington station, the depot was originally established by the York & North Midland Railway in 1846. Before the turn of the century, the North Eastern Railway upgraded the facilities with the erection of a three-track shed and this remained in use until 1958. Around this time, Raven B16 Class 4-6-0 no. 61471 has been captured in sidings at the shed. Photograph by Bill Reed.

Above BRIDLINGTON SHED

A group of locomotives stand outside Bridlington shed on 19th May 1964. On the left is Stanier Class 5 4-6-0 no. 45223 which was allocated to Bangor at this time. In the centre is Thompson B1 Class no. 61115 of Bradford Low Moor, whilst on the right is another Stanier Class 5, no. 45219 of Royston. Photograph by Richard Postill.

Below BRIDLINGTON

View south west from the lineside on the approach to Bridlington station as Gresley K3 Class 2-6-0 no. 61957 passes with an express in August 1962. Photograph by Richard Postill.

Above BROUGHTON LANE SIDINGS

On a frigid-looking 3rd February 1963, Robinson O4/8 2-8-0 no. 63683 takes a mixed freight train out of Broughton Lane Sidings, Attercliffe, Sheffield. Photograph by Geoff Warnes.

Below BURTON AGNES STATION

The peace of Burton Agnes station is momentarily broken by Stanier Class 5 no. 44694 rushing through with a Bridlington to Bradford excursion on 5th August 1967. Photograph by Revd J. David Benson courtesy A1 Steam Trust.

Above CADEBY COLLIERY

Cadeby Colliery was located to the west of Doncaster and connected with the line to Sheffield. NCB 0-6-0ST no. 35 was built by Andrew Barclay in 1923 and served several collieries before arriving at Cadeby around 1970. Pictured there during the year, the engine was scrapped at the pit in 1973. Photograph by John Law.

Below BROOKHOUSE

On the South Yorkshire Joint Railway line at Brookhouse with a short coal train on 9th May 1964 is Robinson O4/8 Class no. 63688. Photograph by Geoff Warnes.

Above CALVERLEY AND RODWELL STATION

A train of empty mineral wagons is led southward through Calverley and Rodwell station on 29th June 1963 with Fowler 4F Class no. 44044 at the head. Photograph by Gerald T. Robinson.

Below CANKLOW SHED

Deeley 0F 0-4-0T no. 41528, 0F 0-4-0ST no. 47001 and Johnson 1F 0-6-0T no. 41835 are out of service at Canklow Shed on 19th February 1967. All three had been withdrawn from Langwith Junction at the end of 1966. Photograph by Geoff Warnes.

Above CANKLOW SHED

The LMSR commissioned Kitson & Co. to produce five 0-4-0ST locomotives for shunting duties in the early 1930s. Another five were subsequently ordered under BR in the early 1950s, with no. 47005 – seen here at Canklow shed on 19th February 1967 – the first to enter service in October 1953 to Birkenhead. Photograph by Geoff Warnes.

Below CARNABY STATION

Stanier Class 5 no. 44964 is heading through Carnaby station towards Bridlington with an excursion from Bradford on 5th August 1967. Photograph by Revd J. David Benson courtesy A1 Steam Trust.

Above DENABY CROSSING

The main line between Doncaster and Sheffield passed by Denaby Main Colliery and required a level crossing over Doncaster Road which until relatively recently caused a headache for road users. Traffic has been stopped for an unidentified WD 'Austerity' to trundle eastwards during the 1960s. Photograph by Geoff Warnes.

Below DARFIELD COLLIERY

Darfield No. 1 was delivered to the colliery (south east of Barnsley) new from Hunslet Engine Co. in 1953. Just two years later, the engine was transferred to Houghton Main Colliery a short distance away, only to return in 1959. Pictured at Darfield in May 1971, *Darfield No. 1* was sold three years later. Photograph by Bill Reed.

Above DENABY (LOWFIELD JUNCTION)
Robinson J11/5 Class 0-6-0 no. 64283 has been captured at Denaby on 30th October 1958 passing Lowfield Junction, which saw a branch from the Hull & Barnsley line join the Doncaster-Sheffield route. Photograph by Geoff Warnes.

Below DENABY CROSSING
O4 Class no. 63648 passes over Denaby Crossing c. 1960. Photograph courtesy John Law.

Above DODWORTH COLLIERY
Built for the War Department in 1943, this Hunslet 0-6-0ST (works no. 2857) subsequently worked at Dodworth Colliery (near Barnsley) until transferred to Cadley Hill Colliery in the mid-1970s. The engine is at Dodworth in August 1971. Photograph by Bill Reed.

Below DODWORTH COLLIERY
Hudswell Clarke-built 0-4-0ST *H.C. No. 1* spent seven years at Dodworth Colliery, arriving from Monk Bretton in 1968. Photograph by Bill Reed.

DONCASTER STATION

Thompson A2/3 Class Pacific no. 60513 *Dante* departs from Doncaster station with an express for London on 9th August 1959. Photograph by Geoff Warnes.

Above DONCASTER STATION

View north west from St James's Bridge to Doncaster station and the works c. 1960 as Gresley V2 Class 2-6-2 no. 60914 gathers speed with a southbound express. The locomotive was an early withdrawal in September 1962. Photograph by Geoff Warnes.

Below DONCASTER STATION

A slow train to Cleethorpes leaves Doncaster station during the late 1950s with Robinson D11/1 Class 4-4-0 no. 62660 *Butler-Henderson*. A V2 can be seen on standby in the background, as can the Great Northern Railway-built goods shed. Photograph by Geoff Warnes.

Above DONCASTER STATION

No. 68800 has come to grief at the north end of Doncaster station during April 1955. The engine originally belonged to LNER Class J53 but was rebuilt in September 1930 to become J52/1. Photograph by Geoff Warnes.

Below DONCASTER STATION

A local service arrives at Doncaster station during August 1966 with Stanier Class 5 no. 45063 of Leeds Holbeck shed. Photograph by Les Flint courtesy John Law.

Above DONCASTER STATION
On 11th July 1966 a train from Leeds stands at Doncaster station's platform four. Armstrong Whitworth-built Stanier Class 5 no. 45211 waits to move forward. Photograph by Geoff Warnes.

Below DONCASTER SHED
Thompson A1/1 Class Pacific no. 60113 *Great Northern* shows up a line of otherwise drab locomotives at Doncaster shed during 1958. Photograph by Geoff Warnes.

DONCASTER STATION
Holden B12 Class 4-6-0 no. 61553 heads south away from Doncaster station as Robinson O4 Class 2-8-0 no. 63798 approaches with a through freight on 29th June 1955. Photograph by Geoff Warnes.

Above DONCASTER STATION
An atmospheric view of Stanier 'Jubilee' Class no. 45739 *Ulster* at Doncaster station as the engine stands at the head of an evening parcels service on 26th March 1966. The engine was Wakefield-allocated at this time. Photograph by Geoff Warnes.

Below DONCASTER WORKS
The cutters have been busy at Doncaster Works as all that remains of Gresley J39 Class 0-6-0 no. 64970 is the smokebox. Pictured on 4th June 1961, the engine had been condemned just two weeks earlier. Photograph by Ron Fisher.

DONCASTER ST JAMES' BRIDGE STATION

The LNER opened Doncaster St James's Bridge station to the south west of Doncaster station in 1930, mainly to serve visitors to the town's racecourse, although some other excursion traffic was accommodated. Robinson C13 Class 4-4-2T no. 67411 is passing the station with a local service on 31st August 1954. Photograph by Geoff Warnes.

Above DONCASTER SHED
A 500-ton mechanical coaler was installed at Doncaster as part of a modernisation of the depot's facilities shortly after Grouping. This was in use until the shed closed to steam in April 1966 and stood until early 1970 when demolition was carried out. Photograph by Geoff Warnes.

Below DONCASTER STATION
View south from St James's Bridge with Gresley A3 Class Pacific no. 60110 *Robert the Devil* approaching with an express on 26th September 1954. Photograph by Geoff Warnes.

Above DORE AND TOTLEY STATION
Johnson 2P Class 4-4-0 no. 40337 pilots Stanier 'Jubilee' Class no. 45602 *British Honduras* near Dore and Totley station on 9th October 1954. Photograph by Geoff Warnes.

Below DORE AND TOTLEY STATION
A southbound express sweeps through Dore and Totley station behind Stanier 'Jubilee' no. 5628 *Somaliland*. Photograph courtesy John Law.

Above DRIFFIELD

Thompson B1 no. 61319 has been caught near Driffield with a summer Saturday express from Filey Holiday Camp. Photograph by Gerald T. Robinson.

Below DUNFORD BRIDGE

Normally assigned shunting duties at Wath Marshalling Yard, Robinson S1 Class (GCR 8H) 0-8-4T no. 69901 has ventured away on 1st August 1950, being captured at Dunford Bridge amidst construction work for the new Woodhead Tunnel. The engine has likely been at Gorton for repairs. Photograph by B.W.L. Brooksbank.

Above DUNFORD BRIDGE STATION

A train of up empties has emerged from Woodhead Tunnel at Dunford Bridge on 25th April 1950 with Peppercorn K1 2-6-0 no. 62020 leading. New to Gorton shed in August 1949, a transfer to March shed occurred in May 1950. Photograph by B.W.L. Brooksbank.

Opposite above DUNFORD BRIDGE STATION

The Thompson O1 Class 2-8-0 was produced to replace all 2-8-0s and some 0-6-0s then in use by the LNER and was to use the diagram 100A boiler fitted to the B1 Class, as well as the cylinders, and the pony truck from the L1 2-6-4T. Several Robinson O4 Class 2-8-0s were subsequently rebuilt, taking the O1 classification, which eventually only consisted of rebuilds numbering 58. One of this number is at Dunford Bridge station on 26th April 1950 – no. 63784. The locomotive had been purchased in 1925 and was rebuilt in June 1944. Photograph by B.W.L. Brooksbank.

Opposite below DUNFORD BRIDGE STATION

A combination of factors resulted in the construction of a third tunnel connecting Dunford Bridge and Woodhead on the Sheffield-Manchester line. The condition of the two tunnels then in use was deteriorating, especially the first, whilst the LNER's electrification scheme would not have sufficient space to be installed in the existing structures. Work began in the late 1940s and was completed during 1953, with the three-mile-long tunnel opened in the following year. Materials are assembled at Dunford Bridge station on 24th December 1949 – tracks and wagons for removing the spoils – as Robinson O4 no. 63771 passes through with a freight train. Photograph by B.W.L. Brooksbank.

FILEY STATION

The Stephenson and Manchester Locomotive Societies' joint organised tour of the Whitby Moors has made a stop at Filey Holiday Camp on 6th March 1965. 'Peppercorn' Class A2 No. 62005 was partnered with preserved Gresley K4 No. 3442 *The Great Marquess* for part of the journey. Photograph by Richard Postill.

Above ELSECAR

The Sheffield branch of the RCTS organised a railtour around South Yorkshire for 7th June 1953. Robinson J11/5 no. 64374 was one of three locomotives used and worked just a short portion of the trip on the Elsecar branch. Photograph by Geoff Warnes.

Below FILEY HOLIDAY CAMP

The first Butlin's holiday camp was built at Skegness in 1936 and Butlin was expanding with another at Filey before the Second World War broke out. Eventually completed in 1945, the camp was reached via a spur of the line to Scarborough and had a dedicated station. Raven B16 Class 4-6-0 no. 61476 departs from there with the 09.40 for Sheffield Victoria on 29th July 1961. The station managed to survive until the mid-1970s and Filey camp closed in 1983. Photograph by Gerald T. Robinson.

FRYSTON COLLIERY
Located to the north east of Castleford,
Fryston Colliery was sunk in the early
1870s and was operational until 1985.
Fryston No. 2 (built by Hudswell Clarke
in 1955) is at work there during 1971.
Photograph by Bill Reed.

Above GLASSHOUGHTON COLLIERY
Hunslet Engine Co. 0-6-0ST *GH No. 4* worked at both Glasshoughton Colliery and the coking plant during 19 years in service. The engine was later preserved. Photograph by Bill Reed.

Below GRIMETHORPE COLLIERY
Out of service minus rods at Grimethorpe Colliery is *No. 4*. Built in 1945, the engine was refurbished in 1966 and was operational until 1972. Photograph by Bill Reed.

Above GOLDTHORPE

Located approximately mid-way between Barnsley and Doncaster, the village of Goldthorpe had three railway lines pass through thanks to the large number of collieries in the area. The Swinton & Knottingley Joint Railway was the first to open from Ferrybridge, near Pontefract, to Swinton in the 1870s, followed by the Hull & Barnsley Railway's branch from Wrangbrook Junction to Wath at the turn of the century. The final route was the Dearne Valley Railway, which ran between Brierley Junction (H&BR) and Black Carr Junction (GNR), and began services in 1909. The DVR was operated by the Lancashire & Yorkshire Railway as the company also made a connection near Brierley Junction at Shafton Junction with the line from Wakefield. WD 'Austerity' Class 2-8-0 no. 90430 has charge of a train of coal wagons on the line at Goldthorpe on 4th March 1966. The engine had entered service in the North East just before Nationalisation and had spells at depots in that area and Hull before arriving at Wakefield in early 1963. No. 90430 had just over four years at the shed before a brief stint at Normanton was completed prior to withdrawal in September 1967. Photograph by Geoff Warnes.

Opposite GOLDTHORPE

WD 'Austerity' 2-8-0 no. 90654 entered service following overhaul at Crewe Works in May 1949 and was allocated to Wakefield shed. The engine subsequently resided there until condemned in June 1967. A number of the WD 2-8-0s employed at the depot received a white circle painted on to the cab side to signify that they were capable of working coal trains on the Dearne Valley line as these were quite tightly timed and also offered financial incentives to the crews that worked them. No. 90654, which is on the line at Goldthorpe on 4th March 1966, had last been overhauled at Darlington in June 1965 and was evidently still in good condition, although the sanders are on to help the engine progress. Photograph by Geoff Warnes.

Above and Opposite GOLDTHORPE AND THURNSCOE HALT

The driver, guard and passengers of this auto-train are all smiles at Goldthorpe and Thurnscoe Halt on 9th September 1951, despite this being the last day of passenger services on the Dearne Valley Railway line. Incorporated in 1897 the company was promoted in the interests of the many collieries lying on the proposed route from the Hull & Barnsley Railway line south east of Wakefield to the Great Northern Railway main line and the Great Northern & Great Eastern Joint line south of Doncaster. Discussions were held with these companies to run the completed line but the DVR eventually chose the Lancashire & Yorkshire Railway, which was obliged to lay a connection from Crofton to Shafton Junction (east of Cudworth), although other companies had running powers. The line opened in stages beginning in 1902 and was not operational along the entire length until 1909. A passenger service did not begin until 3rd June 1912 when a railmotor left Wakefield at 08.15 and terminated at Edlington for Balby Halt (west of Doncaster centre). The other stops on the line were also halts and located at Ryhill, Grimethorpe, Great Houghton, Goldthorpe and Thurnscoe, Harlington and Denaby. Usage was always light and in the austerity years following the Second World War the service was axed. Interestingly, the original motor coach was in use until the end, although converted to 'push and pull' haulage by steam locomotive. Latterly this was done by an Ivatt Class 2MT 2-6-2T and no. 41284 heads the service seen here on both pages. The locomotive had entered service to Wakefield just a year earlier and would end its life at Nine Elms in the Southern Region during early 1967. The first closure of a portion of the DVR had occurred a year earlier and continued into the 1970s; the final section left ran from Black Carr Junction to Yorkshire Main, Edlington. The above photograph is reproduced courtesy of *Yorkshire Post Newspapers*; the one opposite was taken by Geoffrey Oates.

Above GOOLE

No. 51361 began life as part of L&YR Locomotive Superintendent W. Barton Wright's Class 25 0-6-0 locomotives in February 1878 but was later rebuilt by Aspinall as an 0-6-0ST in July 1893. The engine remained in service to October 1956 and has been pictured here at Goole on 1st August 1953. Photograph by Geoff Warnes.

Below GOOLE

A group of enthusiasts on a visit to Goole – likely the shed – have clambered aboard Ivatt Class 2MT 2-6-0 no. 46408 on 24th Jan 1954. Photograph by Geoff Warnes.

Above GOOLE STATION

Selby-allocated Worsdell G5 Class 0-4-4T no. 67286 is with a local service at Goole station during July 1950. The engine survived until October 1956. Photograph by Geoffrey Oates.

Below GRIMETHORPE COLLIERY SIDINGS

Ivatt 2MT 2-6-2T no. 41250 has stopped to take on water at Grimethorpe Colliery Sidings during August 1951. Photograph by Geoffrey Oates.

Above GOOLE SHED

A trio of WD 'Austerity' Class 2-8-0s are inside Goole shed on 11th August 1963. Two are identifiable: closest to the camera is no. 90260 and behind is no. 90228. Both engines were just a short time away from withdrawal. Photograph by Philip Jackson courtesy A1 Steam Trust.

Opposite above HARROGATE STATION

Empty stock for the 'Yorkshire Pullman' service arrives at Harrogate station c. 1960 with BR Standard Class 4 2-6-4T no. 80117 leading. Although the roots of the train were formed in the 1920s, the 'Yorkshire Pullman' began in 1935 and ran from King's Cross to Harrogate, with portions for Hull and Bradford. By the 1960s the train left Harrogate at 10.07 and would reach the capital at 14.38, with the reverse travelling from 17.30 until 21.56. Photograph by Revd J. David Benson courtesy A1 Steam Trust.

Opposite below HALIFAX STATION

Aspinall 27 Class 0-6-0 no. 52400 has been captured at Halifax during the late 1950s. Displaying Bradford Hammerton Street depot's '56G' shedcode, the engine was condemned there in November 1960. Photograph courtesy Colour-Rail.

HARROGATE STARBECK SHED

Starbeck shed was established by the NER in 1857 to the south of Starbeck station and east of Harrogate town centre. Stanier 4P Class 2-6-4T no. 42477 is in front of the building during a brief allocation lasting between January and June 1959. Photograph by Bill Reed.

Above HARROGATE STATION
A train of empty stock arrives at Harrogate station with Gresley D49/2 Class 4-4-0 no. 62749 *The Cottesmore* on 29th November 1951. Photograph courtesy *Yorkshire Post Newspapers*.

Below HARROGATE STATION
New Ivatt Class 2MT 2-6-0 no. 46485 passes through Harrogate station on 29th November 1951, interestingly connected to an NER tender. Photograph courtesy *Yorkshire Post Newspapers*.

Above HARROGATE STATION

Shunting operations at Harrogate station came to a dramatic conclusion on 8th August 1956. A light engine collided with a horse box and this carriage sending the latter down a 70 ft embankment and into the front room of Mr and Mrs Kirby of Nydd Vale Terrace. Luckily, they were in the rear kitchen at the time and their son and his friend had also just gone from the front of the house to the back to repair a punctured bike tyre. Photograph courtesy *Yorkshire Post Newspapers*.

Opposite above HARROGATE STARBECK SHED

Gresley J39 Class 0-6-0 no. 64847 was erected at Darlington Works in May 1933 and worked for the next twenty years in the North East at Heaton, Darlington and Middlesbrough. No. 64847 was then transferred to Harrogate Starbeck shed and spent six years there. The engine is pictured shortly before moving on to Selby in June 1959. Spells at York and Sunderland brought no. 64847's career to an end in November 1962. Photograph by Bill Reed.

Opposite below HARROGATE STATION

The Leeds to Thirsk line originally bypassed Harrogate when built in the late 1840s and the station for Harrogate was at Starbeck several miles to the east of the town. This was because the route chosen by the Leeds Northern Railway wanted to avoid difficult terrain which was encountered at Harrogate. After the line was taken over by the North Eastern Railway, the company took up the challenge and opened a line to the town on 1st August 1862, with a station designed by noted architect Thomas Prosser. Harrogate station has a Liverpool to Newcastle express drawing up to the platform here on 29th November 1951. The train is double headed by Gresley D49/2 Class 4-4-0 no. 62753 *The Belvoir* and Thompson B1 Class 4-6-0 no. 61069. Photograph courtesy *Yorkshire Post Newspapers*.

Above HATFIELD COLLIERY

Hudswell Clarke 0-6-0ST *Hatfield No. 6* arrived at Hatfield Colliery in late 1950 from Appleby-Frodingham steel works, Scunthorpe. The engine was subsequently scrapped on site at the end of 1969. Photograph by Geoff Warnes.

Below HARROGATE STATION

Gresley J39 Class 0-6-0 no. 64855 (with ex-NER tender) leads WD 'Austerity' Class 2-8-0 no. 90426 through Harrogate station with a freight train on 29th November 1951. Photograph courtesy *Yorkshire Post Newspapers*.

Above HATFIELD COLLIERY
Built in 1909 by Hawthorn Leslie & Co., 0-6-0ST *Hatfield No. 1* was on site at Nationalisation in 1947 and would be scrapped there by the end of the 1960s. Photograph by Geoff Warnes.

Below HAZLEHEAD
Passing under the incomplete electrification gantries at Hazlehead on the 'Woodhead' route is Thompson B1 Class no. 61184. The engine is coupled to the 15.20 Sheffield Victoria to Manchester London Road on 1st August 1950. Photograph by B.W.L. Brooksbank.

Above HAYBURN WYKE STATION
Located between Scarborough and Whitby, Hayburn Wyke station was opened by the railway company of that name in mid-July 1885 and was open, with a gap during the First World War, until 1965. The station is pictured during 1968 with the track still extant, but this was later cleared and the station became a private house. Photograph by Revd J. David Benson courtesy A1 Steam Trust.

Below HEBDEN BRIDGE
Hughes 'Crab' Class 2-6-0 no. 42715 travels eastward with an empty coal train near Hebden Bridge on 10th June 1959. Photograph by B.W.L. Brooksbank.

Above HAZLEHEAD

A loaded coal train is dragged up towards Woodhead by Gresley J39 Class no. 64745 on 1st August 1950. Photograph by B.W.L. Brooksbank.

Below HELLIFIELD SHED

BR Standard Class 7 'Britannia' Pacific no. 70041 *Sir John More* has the attention of enthusiasts at Hellifield shed. Photograph by John Law.

Above HELLIFIELD STATION

When promoted in the mid-1840s, the 'Little' North Western Railway promised an ambitious scheme to connect West Yorkshire with the North West and Scotland. Yet, owing to financial pressures the project had to be scaled back and the first section of line from Skipton came to a halt at Ingleton in 1849. The company then decided to push on to Lancaster and this section was ready for traffic by the end of the year. Hellifield station was opened during mid-1849 and was originally just a small facility serving the village. In 1880 a new, larger station was built by the Midland Railway as part of the Settle-Carlisle project and as a result of the formation of a new connection made by the completion of the Lancashire & Yorkshire Railway's line from Blackburn. Despite the initial importance of the station, this subsequently dwindled and following the closure of the latter line Hellifield fell into disrepair even after being listed in the mid-1970s. Yet, the station has been revived over the last 20 years and continues to see regular services. Here, on 27th May 1967, Stanier 'Jubilee' Class 4-6-0 no. 45675 *Hardy* departs Hellifield for Leeds with a parcels train. Photograph by Revd J. David Benson courtesy A1 Steam Trust.

Above HEMSWORTH EAST JUNCTION

The Railway Correspondence & Travel Society's jaunt around South Yorkshire on 7th June 1953 would begin the final leg after Robinson D11/1 Class 4-4-0 no. 62667 *Somme* had backed on to the train at Hemsworth East Junction. Ex-H&BR and ex-GCR lines would be taken as the day ended at Sheffield Midland station. Photograph by Geoff Warnes.

Below HEXTHORPE

A local service led by Robinson J11 Class 0-6-0 no. 64398 is on the Doncaster-Sheffield line at Hexthorpe – a suburb of Doncaster located to the south west of the town – on 31st October 1954. Photograph by Geoff Warnes.

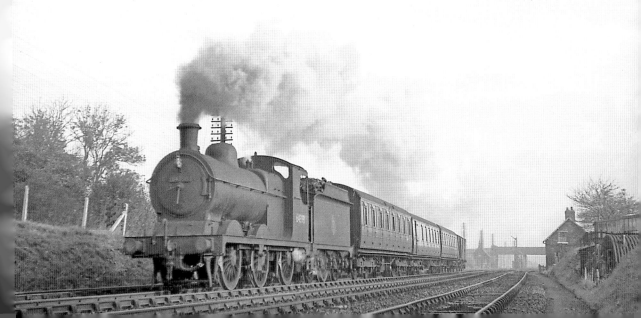

HORBURY AND OSSETT STATION

Stanier 8F Class 2-8-0 no. 48608 approaches Horbury and Ossett station with an eastbound train of flatwagons on 4th July 1963; Healey Mills marshalling yard is in the background. Photograph by Gerald T. Robinson.

Above HEXTHORPE

An express passes through Hexthorpe at speed on 30th April 1955, with Stanier 'Jubilee' Class no. 45590 *Travancore* in charge. Photograph by Geoff Warnes.

Below HEXTHORPE JUNCTION

On a particularly rare visit to South Yorkshire on 12th May 1963 was Bulleid 'West Country' Pacific no. 34094 *Mortehoe*. The engine has been caught at Hexthorpe Junction, which was on the Doncaster-Sheffield line and the point of divergence for the avoiding line, with the Warwickshire Railway Society's special from Birmingham to Doncaster and on the return journey. Photograph by Mick Fowler courtesy John Law.

Above HORTON IN RIBBLESDALE

An unidentified Stanier Class 5 approaches Horton in Ribblesdale with a freight train on 1st June 1964. Some 842 locomotives were erected to the design up to 1951 and by 1964 there were 791 still in traffic. This number reduced to 724 at the start of 1965. Photograph by Revd J. David Benson courtesy A1 Steam Trust.

Below HORTON IN RIBBLESDALE

Another numberless Stanier Class 5 has been captured at Horton in Ribblesdale with a freight on 1st June 1964. 151 classmembers were in service for the last year of steam and 18 have found their way into preservation. Photograph by Revd J. David Benson courtesy A1 Steam Trust.

Above HUDDERSFIELD STATION
Stanier 'Jubilee' Class no. 45695 *Minotaur* takes the platform line at Huddersfield station on 21st May 1960. Photograph courtesy Colour-Rail.

Below HUDDERSFIELD STATION
Ivatt Class 2MT 2-6-2T no. 41255 of Farnley Junction is at Huddersfield station on 22nd June 1961. Photograph courtesy Colour-Rail.

Above HUDDERSFIELD SHED

Aspinall 1008 Class 2-4-2T no. 50865 stands outside Huddersfield shed on 3rd April 1955. The engine had entered traffic in January 1901 and was condemned in October 1958. Photograph courtesy Colour-Rail.

Below HUDDERSFIELD SHED

BR Standard Class 5 4-6-0 no. 73162 had been at work from Huddersfield for nearly a year when pictured at the shed on 23rd August 1959. The engine had only been completed in February 1957 and was condemned in May 1965. Photograph courtesy Colour-Rail.

Above HULL

On 25th July 1964 Thompson B1 no. 61256 heads the 08.40 express from Hull to King's Cross. At the end of the summer the locomotive was transferred from Hull to York and was withdrawn there in November 1965. Photograph by Gerald T. Robinson.

Below HULL BOTANIC GARDENS STATION

Some two-and-a-half years had elapsed from the closure of Hull Botanic Gardens station to this image being captured on 20th May 1967. The site was subsequently cleared and track lifted. Photograph by B.W.L. Brooksbank.

Above HULL DAIRYCOATES SHED
Of the 410 Thompson B1 Class locomotives just 59 were named and these mainly came from species of antelope. No. 61010 *Wildebeeste* is one example and has been captured at Hull Dairycoates shed on 11th August 1963. Photograph by Philip Jackson courtesy A1 Steam Trust.

Opposite above HULL DRAPER'S SCRAPYARD
As one locomotive has met the end at Draper's Scrapyard, Hull, during the mid-1960s another looks on at the horror and awaits the same fate. The engine in question is Fowler 'Royal Scot' 4-6-0 no. 46122 *Royal Ulster Rifleman* which had been condemned at Carlisle Upperby shed in October 1964. Photograph by Revd J. David Benson courtesy A1 Steam Trust.

Opposite below HULL DAIRYCOATES SHED
Stood around the turntable in the roundhouse at Hull Dairycoates shed are Thompson B1 no. 61012 *Puku* and Raven B16 no. 61437. Pictured on 11th August 1963, no. 61012 was in the midst of a six-year spell in Hull, whilst no. 61437 had just a year of life left. Photograph by Philip Jackson courtesy A1 Steam Trust.

Above HULL HESSLE ROAD JUNCTION
Ivatt Class 4MT 2-6-0 no. 43138 travels westward at Hessle Road Junction, Hull, with a train of mineral wagons on 25th July 1964. Photograph by Gerald T. Robinson.

Opposite above HULL HESSLE QUARRY
The north bank of the Humber River at Hessle was rich in deposits of chalk and this was excavated over several centuries. With the arrival of the Hull & Selby Railway in the early 1840s, greater exploitation was possible and output steadily grew. Here, on 4th March 1967, WD 'Austerity' Class 2-8-0 no. 90670 has collected a train of chalk wagons and is leaving for Wilmington Works, which was a short distance across the city to the north east. No. 90670 was based at Hull Dairycoates at this time, having arrived from Selby in October 1956. Moving to Goole in May 1967, the locomotive was condemned just a month later. Photograph by Revd J. David Benson courtesy A1 Steam Trust.

Opposite below HULL KING GEORGE DOCK JUNCTION
Towards the end of the 1800s the people of Hull thought that growth of the port was being stunted by the North Eastern Railway, which was the primary company in the area, as facilities in the North East were favoured. This resulted in the formation of the Hull, Barnsley & West Riding Junction Railway & Dock Company (later abbreviated to the Hull & Barnsley Railway) to exploit the export coal traffic in the early 1880s. With the success of this venture, the NER was obliged to offer better facilities and a new dock was promoted at the turn of the century. In the event the rival companies had to work together for the dock – eventually King George Dock – to be built. Opened in 1914, access was gained off the NER's line to Withernsea, whilst there was also a connection to the H&BR's Alexandra Dock located to the west. WD 'Austerity' Class no. 90272 is seen at King George Dock Junction, which led to the Withernsea line, with oil tanker train on 1st March 1967. Photograph by Revd J. David Benson courtesy A1 Steam Trust.

Above HULL SPRINGBANK SOUTH JUNCTION

Travelling southward to Hull Dairycoates at Springbank South Junction on the ex-H&BR line is J94 Class 0-6-0ST no. 68042. Pictured in late February 1963, the engine survived until the end of the year. Photograph by Revd J. David Benson courtesy A1 Steam Trust.

Opposite above HULL PARAGON STATION

The original passenger terminus at Hull was the Hull & Selby Railway's Manor House Street station which was located quite near to the Humber and the docks. Subsequently, trains from the York & North Midland and Manchester & Leeds Railways made connections at Selby increasing the traffic to the station. With the opening of the H&SR route to Bridlington in the mid-1840s thoughts turned to providing a new station north of Manor House and closer to the centre. The Y&NMR had taken over the H&SR by this point and oversaw the project which was completed in 1847. Noted architect G.T. Andrews produced the designs for Hull Paragon station and this consisted of a trainshed over two platforms with Italian Renaissance-style main building and hotel, with the latter being completed a short time later. Modifications were subsequently made in the 1870s and 1880s, but a major rebuilding project was undertaken in the early 20th century and the trainshed was replaced. This can be partially glimpsed here as Gresley D49/1 Class 4-4-0 no. 62701 *Derbyshire* gets away with an express on 5th April 1957; note the carriage sidings on the left, particularly the six-wheeler connected to the Pullman car. Photograph by B.W.L. Brooksbank.

Opposite below HULL HESSLE ROAD JUNCTION

At the extreme southern end of the line to Bridlington and Scarborough was Hessle Road Junction where the route split east and west to the western docks and Selby respectively. Passing the signalbox controlling the junction here on 25th July 1964 is Ivatt 4MT no. 43079 which has a train of loaded coal wagons. Photograph by Gerald T. Robinson.

Above KILNHURST
View southward from Hooton Road, Kilnhurst (north east of Rotherham), as a northbound train of flat wagons approaches behind an unidentified Thompson O1 2-8-0 on 13th March 1955. Photograph by Geoff Warnes.

Below KILDWICK AND CROSSHILLS STATION
Stanier Class 5 no. 44987 passes through Kildwick and Crosshills station with the Edinburgh-St Pancras service during the early 1950s. Not named at this time, the train became 'The Waverley' in 1957. Photograph courtesy *Yorkshire Post Newspapers*.

Above KIRK SANDALL

Peppercorn K1 no. 62004 is at Kirk Sandall, north east of Doncaster, with a mineral train. Although allocated in the North East, the engine had several repairs at Doncaster Works and could be being run-in here. Photograph by Geoff Warnes.

Below KIRKSTALL

A Leeds to Ilkley local service headed by Aspinall Class 5 2-4-2T no. 50636 (left) is passed by Stanier 3P Class 2-6-2T no. 40169 which has a York-Bradford train on 24th June 1952. Photograph courtesy *Yorkshire Post Newspapers*.

Above LEEDS CITY STATION

On 31st January 1965 Stanier Class 5 no. 44838 is heading an eastbound express at Leeds City station. Photograph by Revd J. David Benson courtesy A1 Steam Trust.

Opposite above KNOTTINGLEY STATION

Momentarily stopped at Knottingley station on 1st February 1964, Peppercorn K1 2-6-0 no. 62062 is back underway with a coal train. The station was opened by the Wakefield, Pontefract & Goole Railway in April 1848 and later saw connections with several other lines, such as those to Doncaster, York and Leeds. Knottingley was also the departure point for the Swinton & Knottingley Joint line opened by the NER and MR companies. In addition to local collieries dispatching their products, the station would also see coal traffic for the nearby Ferrybridge power station. Photograph by Revd J. David Benson courtesy A1 Steam Trust.

Opposite below LEEDS HOLBECK SHED

Visiting Fowler 'Crab' Class 2-6-0 no. 42938 is in the yard at Leeds Holbeck shed during 1963 with resident Ivatt Class 2MT 2-6-2T no. 41267. The latter arrived new from Crewe Works in August 1950 and was condemned there in November 1962, whilst the former mainly worked in the Lancashire area, with spells at Stockport, Longsight, Gorton, Lancaster and Newton Heath before withdrawal in September 1965. Also of interest in the yard are the snowploughs which would have been called into action on the lines over the high ground in the area. Photograph by John Briggs courtesy A1 Steam Trust.

Opposite above LEEDS CITY STATION

Stanier Class 5 no. 44951 is in demand for photographs from several enthusiasts at Leeds City station on 4th September 1965. The engine, which has an eastbound express, was working from Mirfield at this time and would have three months at Bradford Low Moor before withdrawal in December 1966. Leeds City station opened in 1938 following the amalgamation of Leeds Wellington and Leeds New stations. Leeds City was soon to undergo rebuilding in 1967. Photograph by Geoff Warnes.

Opposite below LEEDS HOLBECK SHED

A glimpse inside Leeds Holbeck shed on 1st August 1965 reveals long-term residents Stanier Class 5 no. 44852 and Ivatt 4MT 2-6-0 no. 43039, in addition to BR 04 Class 0-6-0 diesel shunter D2243. Photograph by Bill Wright.

Below LEEDS CITY STATION

Travelling westward away from Leeds City station on 19th August 1967 is Stanier 'Jubilee' Class 4-6-0 no. 45562 *Alberta*. The Leeds Holbeck engine, which has the yellow stripe restricting its movement south of Crewe, is coupled to the 06.40 service from Birmingham to Glasgow. Photograph by Gerald T. Robinson.

LEEDS HOLBECK SHED
In the yard at Leeds Holbeck on 21st February 1960 is Stanier 'Jubilee' Class no. 45675 *Hardy*. Photograph by Geoff Warnes.

Above LEEDS HOLBECK SHED

Nestling between a Stanier Class 5 and a diesel shunter is 'Jubilee' Class 4-6-0 no. 45593 *Kolhapur*. Pictured on 19th February 1967, the engine was condemned in October and bought for preservation during 1968. Photograph by Geoff Warnes.

Below LEEDS HOLBECK SHED

Carnforth's Stanier Class 5 no. 45424 is serviced at Leeds Holbeck on a cold-looking 8th January 1967. Note the breakdown crane on the right. Photograph by Geoff Warnes.

LEEDS HOLBECK SHED
'Britannia' Class Pacific no. 70045 *Lord Rowallan* meets a pair of BR Type 4 diesel locomotives – D33 (left) and D396 – at Leeds Holbeck shed on 30th October 1966. Photograph by Bill Wright.

Above LEEDS HOLBECK SHED

Stanier 'Jubilee' Class no. 45647 *Sturdee* is with Stanier Class 5 no. 44854 in Leeds Holbeck shed on 19th February 1967. Photograph by Geoff Warnes.

Below LEEDS HOLBECK SHED

BR Standard Class 4 4-6-0 no. 75023 was coming to the end of a brief allocation to Skipton when pictured at Leeds Holbeck on 8th January 1967 but would survive to the end of steam in August 1968. Photograph by Geoff Warnes.

Above LEEDS CENTRAL STATION

A short train of empty carriages is hauled away from Leeds Central station on 13th April 1963. The engine is Ivatt 2MT 2-6-2T no. 41250 which would be condemned at the end of the year. Photograph by Gerald T. Robinson.

Below LEEDS FARNLEY

Just west of the Leeds city centre at Farnley, Fowler 'Royal Scot' Class 4-6-0 no. 46123 *Royal Irish Fusilier* charges ahead with an express on 8th March 1953. Photograph by Geoff Warnes.

Above **LEEDS NEVILLE HILL**
A Leeds-Scarborough express travels eastward at Neville Hill, Leeds, on 27th November 1957 with Raven B16 Class no. 61475 of York. Photograph courtesy *Yorkshire Post Newspapers*.

Below **LEEDS MARSH LANE**
Thompson B1 no. 61071 is dwarfed by the surroundings of Marsh Lane Cutting, Leeds, on 15th March 1951 as the engine and train approaches City station with an express from Scarborough. Photograph courtesy *Yorkshire Post Newspapers*.

Above MANVERS MAIN COLLIERY

A number of shunting locomotives were required to work at the extensive Manvers Main Colliery, which was spread over two sites. Two former War Department engines are seen here, c. 1969, at work shunting loaded coal wagons. Photograph by John Law.

Opposite above MANNINGHAM SHED

A pair of Ivatt Class 4MT 2-6-0s are out of service at Manningham shed, north of Bradford, on a wintry 8th January 1967. Only the nearest engine is identifiable, no. 43054 which was erected at Doncaster Works in August 1950. No. 43054 was first allocated to Darlington shed but only remained there briefly before moving on to Middlesbrough. By the middle of the decade the locomotive was working at Saltburn, yet in 1957 a brief return to Middlesbrough occurred. This move only lasted until 1958 when transfers were made to Thornaby, Selby and finally Neville Hill before 1960. No. 43054 managed to settle at the latter and had only been a year away at Manningham when pictured here withdrawn only a short time earlier. Photograph by Geoff Warnes.

Opposite below MANNINGHAM SHED

The Leeds & Bradford Railway served Manningham from opening on 1st July 1846. The company was later taken over by the Midland Railway and in the early 1870s the latter decided to establish stabling facilities for locomotives working in the area. A site was chosen on the east side of the line near Manningham station and by 1872 a roundhouse had been erected. This was later supplemented by a straight shed, but this was out of use by Nationalisation in 1948. Just three months remained for the depot before closure when this image was taken inside the roundhouse on 8th January 1967. A trio of Fairburn Class 4P 2-6-4T locomotives are seen in the stalls – no. 42072, no. 42152 and no. 42052 – along with an Ivatt Class 4MT 2-6-0, no. 43051. The latter was just a few weeks from being condemned for scrap, whilst no. 42052 would leave service when the depot closed. No. 42072 and no. 42152 survived for a few more months, being transferred to Wakefield and Leeds before finishing their service lives at Bradford Low Moor Shed in September 1967. Photograph by Geoff Warnes.

MANVERS MAIN COLLIERY
An 0-6-0ST from Manvers Main Colliery moves a mixed train of tipper wagons and hopper wagons over a road crossing on 4th March 1966. Photograph by Geoff Warnes.

Above MEXBOROUGH STATION
WD 'Austerity' no. 90330 heads a train of empty wagons through Mexborough station on 1st July 1963. Photograph by Gerald T. Robinson.

Below MEXBOROUGH STATION
Mexborough station staff pose for the camera during the 1950s. Photograph from author's collection.

Above MILLHOUSES

Hughes 'Crab' Class 2-6-0 no. 42756 heads an express at Millhouses, south of Sheffield, on 21st August 1954. The class was introduced in 1926 for mixed traffic service and some 245 locomotives were erected to the design up to 1932. Of this number 175 were completed at Crewe Works – the others were built at Horwich – and no. 42756 was dispatched into service during June 1927. Photograph by Geoff Warnes.

Opposite above MEXBOROUGH WEST JUNCTION

Just west of Mexborough, which lies between Doncaster and Barnsley, the Swinton & Knottingley Joint line began. This was just north of the ex-Great Central Railway line running from Doncaster to Barnsley and a connection, which can be seen on the left of this image, was made between the two routes via Mexborough West Junction. WD 'Austerity' no. 90340 continues westward with a train of mineral wagons on 1st July 1963. The locomotive had entered service for the LNER during early 1947 at Peterborough and was there for nearly 10 years, moving on to March depot. Arriving at Doncaster shed in November 1961, no. 90340 moved on to Staveley in February 1964 and was withdrawn from there in July 1965. Photograph by Gerald T. Robinson.

Opposite below MILLHOUSES SHED

Shortly after the Midland Railway extended the main line between Derby and Leeds by connecting Sheffield, the company provided a large engine shed with repair facilities at Grimesthorpe, which was to the north of the city. At the turn of the century, another shed was added at Millhouses to the south. This was a large building and covered eight roads which were accessed from the southern end. Initially, the motive power was smaller passenger engines and some goods types, but later larger express locomotives were allocated. One such engine was Fowler Compound 4-4-0 no. 41095 which is at the depot c. 1950. The engine had been erected at Derby Works in August 1925 and was in service until February 1958. Photograph by Geoff Warnes.

Above MIRFIELD
View eastward near Mirfield shed (left, with a Fowler 7F 0-8-0 alongside) as Stanier 'Jubilee' no. 45704 *Leviathan* approaches with the 13.15 express from Leeds City to Manchester Exchange on 27th April 1950. Photograph by B.W.L. Brooksbank.

Below MILLHOUSES
South of Sheffield at Millhouses, Stanier 3P Class 2-6-2T no. 40082 has a local service on 15th March 1952. Photograph by Geoff Warnes.

Above MIRFIELD SHED

WD 'Austerity' Class no. 90351 stands inside Mirfield shed on 17th December 1966. The engine was out of service at this time but would return to steam for spells at Wakefield and Normanton before withdrawal in September 1967. Photograph by Geoff Warnes.

Below MIRFIELD SHED

Another view inside Mirfield shed, although slightly earlier in 1966 on 12th November. BR Standard Class 9F 2-10-0 92231 is alongside Stanier Class 5 no. 45208. The 9F had been withdrawn whilst no. 45208 continued into late 1967. Photograph by Geoff Warnes.

Above MIRFIELD SHED

The Manchester & Leeds Railway's first section from Normanton to Hebden Bridge passed through Mirfield when opened in 1840, yet a station for the town was not provided for a further five years. A short time later, lines were established to Bradford and Huddersfield, making Mirfield an important junction. A small shed was established to the east of the station during this period, then a new depot was built by the Lancashire & Yorkshire Railway in 1885. This was sited to the north west of the station and eight tracks were covered. Outside the building on 12th November 1966 is Stanier Class 5 no. 44806 and classmate no. 45208. The aforementioned was visiting from Speke Junction depot, Liverpool, whilst the latter had travelled from Stoke. Mirfield shed was in use until April 1967 and was later demolished. Photograph by Geoff Warnes.

Opposite above MIRFIELD

Whilst many railway companies built 2-8-0 locomotives for freight traffic during the 1910s and 1920s, the LNWR and MR companies, which formed the LMSR, did not and by the 1930s a modern locomotive was required. Stanier produced the 8F Class 2-8-0 design in 1935 and a large number (852) were built up to 1946. The War Department adopted the design early in the war (before developing the 'Austerity' Class) and some 158 were erected for service in the conflict. One of this number was no. 48222 which was completed by the North British Locomotive Company in September 1942. The engine is at Mirfield – passing by the shed – with a westbound coal train on 19th August 1967. No. 48222 was allocated to Royston shed at this time and was withdrawn from there in November. Photograph by Gerald T. Robinson.

Opposite below MIRFIELD

BR Standard Class 5 4-6-0 no. 73053 heads the 12.30 Leeds to Manchester express at Mirfield on 26th August 1967. The engine was working from Patricroft at this time and would be condemned there in March 1968. Photograph by Gerald T. Robinson.

Above NEWMARKET COLLIERY

Located at Stanley, north of Wakefield, Newmarket Colliery was established in 1837 and ran continuously until 1983 when the reserves were just about exhausted. A railway connection was established in 1865 by the Methley Joint Railway – a combined venture by the L&YR and NER – which connected the lines to Pontefract and York with the GNR's line between Wakefield and Leeds. A number of locomotives worked at the site shunting and one is at the pit head. Hunslet Engine Co. Ltd 0-6-0ST *Jubilee* reported for duty from Waterloo Colliery in early 1966 and was in use until 1973 when cut-up at Newmarket. Photograph by Bill Reed.

Opposite above NORTH GAWBER COLLIERY

Whilst many colliery locomotives were christened, this one, which is working at North Gawber Colliery, has been left nameless. The engine was built by Hudswell Clarke in 1952 as works no. 1857 and arrived new to the site, working there until 1975 when preserved. Photograph by Bill Reed.

Opposite below NEWMARKET COLLIERY

Hunslet Engine Co. Ltd 0-6-0ST *Jess* was another locomotive transferred from Waterloo Colliery, but arrival at Newmarket was slightly later in 1968. The engine was also scrapped on site in 1973 after 30 years in operation. Photograph by Bill Reed.

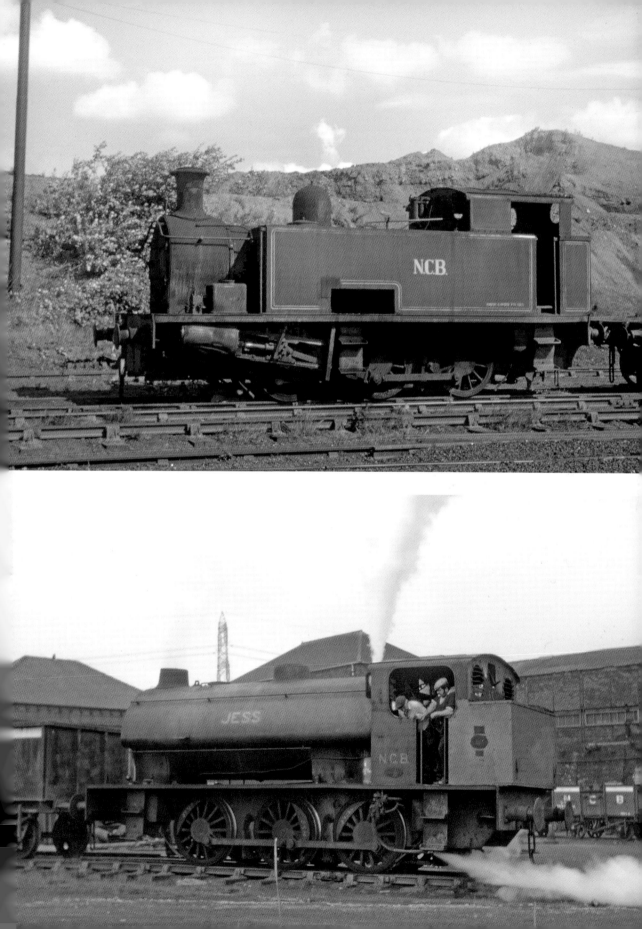

NORMANTON
Peppercorn A1 Class Pacific no. 60146
Peregrine is heading a York to Healey
Mills freight train at Normanton during
April 1965. Photograph by Roger Bastin
courtesy A1 Steam Trust.

Above NORMANTON SHED

On 23rd July 1966 Ivatt 4MT 2-6-0 no. 43044 stands in the shed yard at Normanton. The engine has Stourton's '55B' shedcode painted on to the smokebox door and is missing the front numberplate. Photograph by Gerald T. Robinson.

Below NORMANTON SHED

Ex-L&YR Hughes 31 Class 0-8-0 no. 12928 had a relatively short lifespan, being constructed in March 1919 and withdrawn in September 1947, which was just four months away when pictured here at Normanton shed. Photograph by B.W.L. Brooksbank.

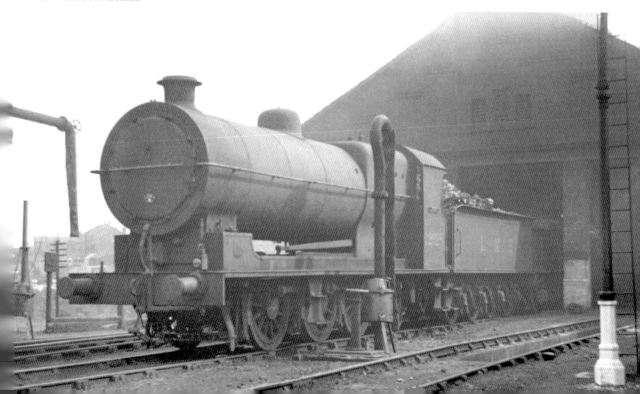

NORMANTON
View north east from just north of Normanton station as Peppercorn K1 Class 2-6-0 no. 62047 trundles along with a freight train on 18th March 1961. Photograph by B.W.L. Brooksbank.

Above NORMANTON STATION
Altofts Road, which straddles the line north of Normanton station, provides the vantage point for this scene, again taken on 18th March 1961. Stanier 'Jubilee' no. 45690 *Leander* has a local service from Sheffield to Leeds. Photograph by B.W.L. Brooksbank.

Below NORTHALLERTON STATION
Gresley A3 Class Pacific no. 60091 *Captain Cuttle* has a train of oil tankers at Northallerton station on 19th April 1963. Photograph by Revd J. David Benson courtesy A1 Steam Trust.

Above ORGREAVE

A Sheffield-bound express passes Orgreave Colliery signal box, which controlled the colliery line on the left, on 16th April 1955. The engine is Gresley B17 Class 4-6-0 no. 61643 *Champion Lodge*. Photograph by Geoff Warnes.

Below PECKFIELD COLLIERY

Hudswell Clarke 0-6-0T no. S100 is at Peckfield Colliery, Micklefield. The engine was dispatched to the site when new in 1949 and remained there until 1973 when preserved. Photograph by Bill Reed.

Above PENISTONE
An unidentified J11 Class 0-6-0 runs tender-first through Penistone with a local service on 27th February 1954. The J11s were designed by J.G. Robinson for the GCR (as 9J) and introduced in 1901 for freight traffic. By the end of the decade some 174 were in service and the first withdrawal would occur during 1954. Photograph by Geoff Warnes.

Below PENISTONE
Also at Penistone on 27th February 1954 was Parker N5 Class no. 69320. Barnsley-allocated at this time, the locomotive was condemned in October 1959. Photograph by Geoff Warnes.

ROTHERHAM MASBOROUGH STATION

After being held at Rotherham Masborough station with a petrol train on 23rd July 1966, BR Standard Class 9F 2-10-0 no. 92137 has the road and advances southward on the ex-MR main line; the line from Sheffield connected via the curve in the background. Photograph by Geoff Warnes.

Above RIPON STATION
Gresley A3 no. 60036 *Colombo* has a Liverpool to Newcastle express at Ripon station on a snowy 28th December 1962. Photograph by Revd J. David Benson courtesy A1 Steam Trust.

Below ROSSINGTON
South of Doncaster at Rossington, Ivatt J6 Class no. 64270 has a short goods train bound for Misson on 28th December 1954. Photograph by Geoff Warnes.

Above ROYSTON SHED

Out of service at Royston on 21st February 1960 is Fowler 2P Class no. 40581. The engine would probably return to service before withdrawal in October. Photograph by Geoff Warnes.

Below ROYSTON

On 15th September 1967 Stanier 8F 2-8-0 no. 48067 has a relatively short coal train at Royston. Just a month later the engine was condemned. Photograph by Geoff Warnes.

Above SCARBOROUGH STATION

Thompson B1 Class no. 61373 has brought a train from Sheffield to Scarborough during August 1961; the engine had just a year left in service. Photograph by David Dippie.

Below SCARBOROUGH STATION

York-based Thompson B1 no. 61062 gets away from Scarborough station with an express on 15th June 1963. BR Type 2 (later Class 30) diesel locomotive no. D5847 is at the platform. Photograph by Revd J. David Benson courtesy A1 Steam Trust.

Above SCARBOROUGH STATION

Another view of no. 61062 as the engine departs from Scarborough station on 15th June 1963. A diesel is again present, but in this instance is BR Type 4 (Class 40) D387 which is light engine. Photograph by Revd J. David Benson courtesy A1 Steam Trust.

Below SCARBOROUGH SHED

Visitors to Scarborough shed have been caught in August 1961. They are: Raven B16 no. 61434; Gresley V3 no. 67640; Thompson B1 no. 61095. Photograph by David Dippie.

Above SCARBOROUGH STATION
Gresley V3 2-6-2T no. 67640 has been serviced and is now taking an express out of Scarborough station in August 1961. The engine was originally a V1 when built but an increase in boiler pressure saw a reclassification to V3; this had occurred for no. 67640 in December 1960. Photograph by David Dippie.

Below SCARBOROUGH STATION
Leeds-based Thompson B1 no. 61123 leaves Scarborough station with an express during August 1961. Photograph by David Dippie.

Above SEAMER JUNCTION

Thompson B1 no. 61069 approaches Seamer Junction with an express on 25th August 1962. Photograph by Richard Postill.

Below SEAMER STATION

A Scarborough to York express passes through Seamer station behind Thompson B1 no. 61161 on 25th August 1962. Photograph by Richard Postill.

Above SELBY STATION
A southbound freight sails through Selby station with Peppercorn A1 Pacific no. 60149 *Amadis* on 2nd March 1963. Photograph by Revd J. David Benson courtesy A1 Steam Trust.

Below SELBY
Only partially identified Worsdell D20 Class 4-4-0 no. 6237? travels over the swing bridge at Selby c. 1955. Photograph by Geoff Warnes.

Above SELBY SHED

Raven B16 Class no. 61459 had just two years displaying Selby depot's '50C' shedcode from June 1957 to June 1959. The engine is in the yard during this period. Photograph by Bill Reed.

Below SETTLE JUNCTION

Fowler 4F no. 43893 joins the Settle-Carlisle line at Settle Junction with a train of empty ammonia tankers from Heysham to Billingham on 22nd September 1962. Photograph by B.W.L. Brooksbank.

Above SELBY STATION
Worsdell J21 Class no. 65105 has a train at Selby station during June 1950. The engine would be withdrawn 15 months later. Photograph by Geoffrey Oates.

Below SHEFFIELD MIDLAND STATION
The 16.31 service to Chinley departs from Sheffield Midland station behind Thompson B1 no. 61153 on 2nd July 1963. Photograph by Gerald T. Robinson.

Above SHEFFIELD VICTORIA STATION

Sheffield Victoria station was completed in 1851 replacing the Sheffield, Ashton-under-Lyne & Manchester Railway's original terminus opened in 1845. The station was subsequently modified several times, lastly for the Woodhead electrification scheme. Thompson B1 no. 61182 stands under the wires at the station, c. 1955. Photograph by Geoff Warnes.

Opposite above SHEFFIELD MIDLAND STATION

This image is interesting for showing, not only the last scheduled steam service between Sheffield and Barnsley, but the Park Hill area to the east of the station before the erection of the complex of flats. Ivatt Class 2MT 2-6-2T no. 41281 has been given the honour of heading the service on 13th June 1959. Working from Royston at this time, around a week later the engine was transferred to Leeds Neville Hill. Sheffield Midland station was opened in 1870 after an extension was built from the original North Midland Railway main line north of Chesterfield. Photograph by Geoff Warnes.

Below SHEFFIELD VICTORIA STATION

In the early 20th century J.G. Robinson attempted to provide the GCR with modern express passenger locomotives, yet these proved unsuccessful. In 1913 he reduced his ambitions somewhat and designed a simple and robust 4-4-0. These were classified 11E (LNER D10) and subsequently followed by the 11F Class (LNER D11) which was slightly modified. Eleven were built before Grouping, then Gresley adopted the design to meet the need for motive power in Scotland and a further 24 were constructed. No. 62660 *Butler-Henderson* was the first of the class to be completed at Gorton Works in December 1919. The engine backs on to a train at Sheffield Victoria station during 1958. Based at Sheffield Darnall from April 1957 until withdrawal in December 1960, no. 62660 was subsequently preserved as part of the National Collection. Photograph by Geoff Warnes.

Above SHEFFIELD MIDLAND STATION

The Warwickshire Railway Society organised a tour over the Settle-Carlisle line for 4th September 1965. Peppercorn A1 no. 60145 *Saint Mungo* collected the party from Birmingham and travelled to Leeds, handing over the reins to no. 4472 *Flying Scotsman*. Here, no. 60145 has made a stop at Sheffield Midland. Photograph by Geoff Warnes.

Below SHEFFIELD VICTORIA STATION

Robinson C13 Class 4-4-2T no. 67424 at Sheffield Victoria during mid-1958. This Darnall engine was withdrawn at the end of the year. Photograph by Geoff Warnes.

Above SHEFFIELD MIDLAND STATION

A train of empty coaching stock arrives at Sheffield Midland station behind Thompson B1 no. 61083 on 2nd July 1963. Photograph by Gerald T. Robinson.

Below SHEFFIELD MIDLAND STATION

No. 61083 appears again at Sheffield Midland on 2nd July 1963 and is now leaving with the 17.30 local service to Manchester. Stanier Class 5 no. 45139 is on the middle road and B1 no. 61334 is at the platform. Photograph by Gerald T. Robinson.

SKIPTON

View west from Carleton New Road as Stanier Class 5 no. 45354 approaches Skipton station with the 07.37 service from Morecambe to Leeds on 1st August 1964. Photograph by Gerald T. Robinson.

Above SKIPTON STATION

'The Waverley' express passes through Skipton on 18th April 1960 with Stanier 'Jubilee' no. 45564 *New South Wales* at the head. Photograph by Geoff Warnes.

Below SKIPTON SHED

View from the turntable at Skipton shed during 1964. Fowler 3F 0-6-0T no. 47599 is on the left and an Ivatt 4MT 2-6-0, possibly no. 43028, stands just outside the shed. Photograph by Les Flint courtesy John Law.

Above SKIPTON

Skipton was originally at the end of the Leeds & Bradford Railway when the line opened in early September 1847. Nearly two years later, the 'Little' North Western Railway extended the tracks to Lancaster and Morecambe and Skipton became a stopping point on a through route. With the promotion of the Settle-Carlisle line in the early 1870s by the Midland Railway, Skipton became a major junction and this required a new station which opened in 1876. Soon after a three-road engine shed and sidings were opened and these are shown here, left and right respectively, in the background as Stanier Class 5 no. 44935 heads as southbound express on 1st August 1964. Photograph by Gerald T. Robinson.

Opposite SKIPTON

At Grouping the Midland Railway's 2441 Class 0-6-0T design was chosen for development as the standard shunting and short distance freight locomotive for the London Midland & Scottish Railway. This was the best candidate from the constituents of the company, possessing many standard components and successful features. Designated 3F and attributed to Fowler, some 422 locomotives were erected at several locations between 1924 and 1931 and spread the length and breadth of the LMSR's system. No. 47428 was constructed by the Hunslet Engine Co. during October 1926 and served until October 1965. In the BR period the locomotive was allocated to Skipton from July 1953 to September 1962 when transferred to Agecroft. Here, no. 47428 has four coal wagons at Skipton on 19th April 1960. Photograph by Geoff Warnes.

Above SOUTH KIRKBY COLLIERY
Hunslet 0-6-0ST no. 9 *Kinsley* arrived at South Kirkby Colliery from New Monkton in 1967. After eight years at work, the engine was preserved. Photograph by Bill Reed.

Below SOUTH KIRKBY COLLIERY
South east of Wakefield, South Kirkby Colliery was connected to the Wakefield-Doncaster line and was also close to the S&KR, as well as the H&BR. Yorkshire Engine Co. 0-4-0ST *York No. 1* worked from South Kirkby from February 1971 and was later preserved in 1975. Photograph by Bill Reed.

Above SOWERBY BRIDGE
WD 'Austerity' Class 2-8-0 no. 90595 passes Sowerby Bridge West signal box with a coal train on 4th July 1963. Photograph by Gerald T. Robinson.

Below STAINFORTH
Despite the frigid conditions of 12th February 1955, cabless Robinson O4 Class 2-8-0 no. 63671 of Frodingham has been turned out to work a mixed freight train and the intrepid cameraman has caught the working at Stainforth, north east of Doncaster. Photograph by Geoff Warnes.

Above STAINFORTH & HATFIELD STATION

A busy scene captured at Stainforth & Hatfield station on 12th March 1966. WD 'Austerity' no. 90707 has a through freight and is passed by a DMU amidst a large number of wagons assembled in the sidings along either side of the line, which split a short distance away to Goole and Scunthorpe, Frodingham and Grimsby. Hatfield Main Colliery is in the background. Photograph by Geoff Warnes.

Below STAINFORTH & HATFIELD STATION

The Gainsborough Model Railway Society's tour of freight lines in South Yorkshire has made a stop at Stainforth & Hatfield station on 12th October 1963; Robinson O4 no. 63585 is the motive power. Photograph by Geoff Warnes.

Above STAITHES STATION

BR Standard Class 4 2-6-4T no. 80118 pauses at Staithes station, c. 1955, on the line between Saltburn and Whitby. Photograph courtesy of Neil Cholmondeley.

Below STAITHES VIADUCT

A local service travels over Staithes viaduct. This was erected in 1875 and stood just over 150 feet above Staithes Beck. When the line closed in 1958, the viaduct was subsequently demolished. Photograph courtesy of Neil Cholmondeley.

Above SWINTON

An unidentified WD 'Austerity' has a freight train at Swinton on 28th May 1960. During the war R.A. Riddles adapted the 8F design to produce a simpler and cost-saving engine. A total of 935 were built, with 733 passing to BR in 1948. Photograph by Geoff Warnes.

Below STILLINGFLEET

Before the East Coast Main Line was diverted north of Selby, the route ran between Stillingfleet and Escrick. Here, 'Austerity' no. 90601 heads southbound with a train of oil tanks on 11th September 1964. Photograph by Revd J. David Benson courtesy A1 Steam Trust.

Above THORNTON-IN-CRAVEN STATION
The 08.19 Barnoldswick to Skipton local service passes through Thornton-in-Craven station with Fowler 4P Class 2-6-4T no. 42394 on 1st August 1964. Photograph by Gerald T. Robinson.

Below WAKEFIELD KIRKGATE STATION
WD 'Austerity' Class no. 90094 and Stanier Class 5 no. 44938 meet at Wakefield Kirkgate station on 22nd July 1965. Photograph by Bill Wright.

Above TINSLEY

Tinsley was just a small village on the north east edge of Sheffield in the early 19th century. With the arrival of the railways, the area was rapidly industrialised to the start of the 1900s with the establishment of collieries and steel works. These concerns were served by several sidings, both large and small; an extensive marshalling yard was established during the 1960s at Tinsley alongside the branch between Brightside and Treeton. Robinson O4/8 Class 2-8-0 no. 63882 has been caught in the Tinsley area on a snowy 21st February 1963, with BR Class 10 diesel shunter D4062 for company. Both were residents of Darnall depot at this time. Photograph by Geoff Warnes.

Above WAKEFIELD KIRKGATE STATION

Stanier 4P Class 2-6-4T no. 42574 stands at platform two with a local service for Bradford Exchange at Wakefield Kirkgate station on 14th January 1967. Photograph by Geoff Warnes.

Below WAKEFIELD KIRKGATE STATION

Four withdrawn Stanier locomotives are hauled through Wakefield Kirkgate station on 17th May 1968. BR Type 3 (later Class 37) diesel D6739 is leading the condemned to Hull, having collected them from sheds in the North West. From front to back they are: 8F no. 48307 (Patricroft); 8F no. 48700 (Patricroft); Class 5 no. 45294 (Bolton); 8F no. 48740 (Bolton). Photograph by Bill Wright.

WAKEFIELD KIRKGATE STATION

View east from Wakefield Kirkgate station on 2nd January 1967 and two WD 'Austerity' Class 2-8-0s – no. 90160 and no. 90631 – are without a train; a freight can be glimpsed disappearing southward. Both locomotives were allocated to Wakefield shed and were approaching the end of their lives, with no. 90631 just days away, whilst no. 90160 survived until July. The area past the signal box was occupied by large sidings and carriage shed, which were subsequently abandoned and the area has returned to nature. Photograph by Bill Wright.

Above WAKEFIELD SHED
On 9th April 1967 Fairburn 4P Class 2-6-4T no. 42269 is out of service – note the damage to the water tank – at Wakefield shed. The engine was withdrawn three months later. Photograph by Gerald T. Robinson.

Below WAKEFIELD WESTGATE STATION
View north from the platform at Wakefield Westgate station on 14th January 1967 as WD 'Austerity' Class no. 90692 leads a coal train past Stanier 4P Class 2-6-4T no. 42574. Photograph by Geoff Warnes.

Above WAKEFIELD KIRKGATE STATION

The North Midland Railway missed several places in Yorkshire, including Wakefield. The closest station to the city on the line was at Oakenshaw, two miles away. With the completion of the Manchester & Leeds Railway, which connected to the NMR at Normanton, Wakefield saw a basic station established at Kirkgate. The Great Northern Railway subsequently attempted to build a line to Wakefield but was thwarted several times and eventually had to enter into an agreement with the Wakefield, Pontefract & Goole Railway. The line was planned to end at Kirkgate and an agreement was reached with the Lancashire & Yorkshire Railway (successor to the M&LR) to build a new station and this was opened in 1857. Fairburn Class 4 2-6-4T no. 42196 is in the station on 29th July 1966, having either uncoupled or preparing to take on the carriages in the distance. Photograph by B.W.L. Brooksbank.

Opposite above WALESWOOD JUNCTION

The Manchester, Sheffield & Lincolnshire Railway's line between Sheffield and Worksop ran just north of the small settlement of Waleswood, near Beighton. Later, a colliery was established in the area, but a station was not provided until 1907. Yet, owing to the remote nature of the colliery and village, Waleswood station was closed in 1955. This image has been captured very close to the station on 4th July 1963 and the camera is looking westward towards Brookhouse Colliery; Waleswood Junction is on the left and this was a spur that connected to the Sheffield branch of the Lancashire, Derbyshire & East Coast Railway, which ran between Chesterfield and Lincoln. Peppercorn K1 Class 2-6-0 no. 62069 is also featured and has an eastbound loaded coal train. Photograph by Gerald T. Robinson.

Opposite below WALESWOOD JUNCTION

Another scene at Waleswood Junction on 4th July 1963. On this occasion Gresley O2 Class 2-8-0 no. 63980 has a westbound coal train. Photograph by Gerald T. Robinson.

Above WATH ROAD JUNCTION
A train of 20-ton high sided coke wagons heads southward at Wath Road Junction behind Stanier 8F 2-8-0 no. 48060. The locomotive was one of 69 classmembers erected by the Vulcan Foundry, Newton-le-Willows, between 1936 and 1937, entering service in October 1936. No. 48060 spent the majority of the 1950s working from Westhouses depot (north of Alfreton), but had several moves during the 1960s, with spells at Toton, Derby, Kettering and Colwick. The locomotive's final allocation was to Speke Junction and almost 18 months elapsed before withdrawal in April 1968. Photograph by B.W.L. Brooksbank.

Opposite above WARMSWORTH QUARRY
0-4-0ST locomotive *Progress* is at Warmsworth Quarry, south west of Doncaster, on 22nd April 1951. Photograph by Geoff Warnes.

Opposite below WATH ROAD JUNCTION
In the 1870s the North Eastern and Midland Railway companies joined forces to build a line from the old North Midland Railway route near Wath and the line to York. The line was completed in May 1878 and departed from the ex-NMR route at Wath Road Junction. This is the point which Johnson 3F 0-6-0 no. 43714 has been captured with a freight train on 17th June 1957. The locomotive, which had been erected by Neilson, Reid & Co. during 1901, was a long-term resident of Normanton depot and was condemned there in January 1962. Photograph by B.W.L. Brooksbank.

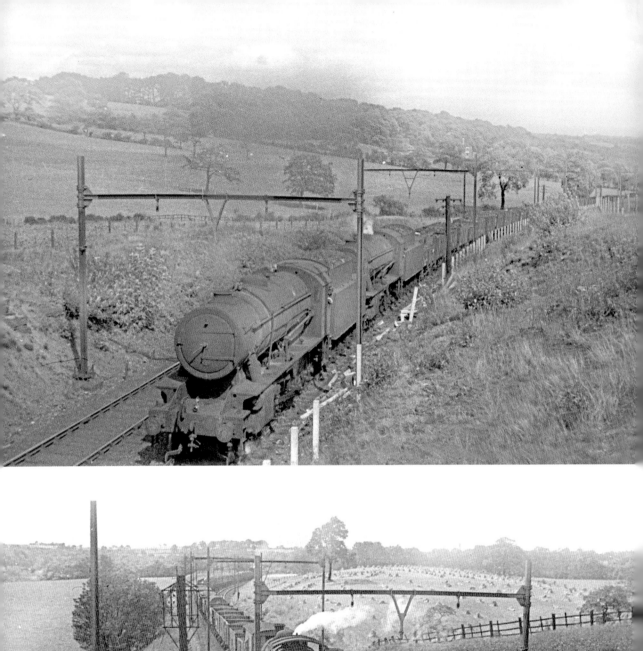

Above WHELDALE COLLIERY

Located just to the east of Castleton, Wheldale Colliery was sunk in 1868 and started raising coal two years later; production continued through to 1987. Hunslet Engine Co. 0-6-0ST – works no. 2879 – is moving some wagons during September 1971. The locomotive was a recent addition to the workforce and would spend a short time at Wheldale, moving on to Newmarket Colliery in late 1973. Photograph by Bill Reed.

Opposite above WORSBROUGH

The Manchester Sheffield & Lincolnshire Railway reached Barnsley from Penistone in mid-1854. A station – Barnsley Exchange – was shared with several other companies, including the South Yorkshire Railway, for a number of years before the MS&LR opened Barnsley Court House in 1870. By this time the company had taken over the SYR which allowed another connection to be made with the east coast through Doncaster. As traffic from nearby collieries increased, Barnsley became a bottleneck for the company. A new route was derived from an old branch to Worsbrough and reached completion in 1880, allowing many coal trains to bypass Barnsley. Yet, the line was one of the most challenging in the country due to steep gradients, including three miles at 1 in 40. Here, a coal train is travelling westward behind two WD 'Austerity' Class locomotives on 11th August 1950. Leading is no. 90190, whilst behind is no. 79242 which still has the WD number and would be renumbered 90696 in early 1951. Photograph by B.W.L. Brooksbank.

Opposite below WORSBROUGH

The coal train shown *Opposite above* has travelled further westward to reveal two bankers that are assisting from the rear. Robinson J11 Class 0-6-0 no. 64374 is behind the brake van and WD 'Austerity' no. 90709 is supporting. Both locomotives were residents of Mexborough shed at this time, as were those leading the train. The Worsbrough branch was electrified along with the Woodhead route during the 1950s and would later close with that line in 1981. Photograph by B.W.L. Brooksbank.

Above WHITBY STATION

Raven Class A8 4-6-2T no. 69861 pilots Thompson B1 Class no. 61143 out of the carriage sidings at Whitby during June 1953. Photograph courtesy Colour-Rail.

Below WHITBY SHED

Thompson B1 no. 61049 is near the two-road shed at Whitby on 4th May 1964. Built by the YNMR in 1847, BR closed the facility in 1959; the building still survives and houses have been erected where the locomotive stands. Photograph courtesy Colour-Rail.

Above WHITBY

Thompson B1 no. 61276 is moved manually on the 60 ft turntable (from 1936) at Whitby during May 1964; the engine was York-based at this time. Photograph courtesy Colour-Rail.

Below WHITBY TOWN STATION

A local service arrives at Whitby Town station during May 1964. Thompson B1 no. 61275 of York is leading. Photograph courtesy Colour-Rail.

Above WILSDEN STATION

The area north west of Bradford proved particularly challenging to railway schemes because of the hilly terrain. Yet, there were certain rewards for the initial high outlay owing to the industry in the area which was not well served otherwise. The Great Northern Railway, with help from the Lancashire & Yorkshire, brought together several schemes and between 1877 and 1884 completed lines from Bradford to Halifax, via the Halifax & Ovenden Junction Railway, and Bradford to Keighley via Queensbury. Wilsden station was on the latter route and not opened until 1886. Here, a local service has stopped at the station c. 1950. Wilsden was closed to passengers in 1955 and freight in late 1963; the line has since been lifted. Photograph David Joy collection.

Opposite above YORK SHED

Sometime during 1967 Stanier 'Jubilee' Class no. 45562 *Alberta* has been captured near York shed's mechanical coaler. The engine was allocated to Leeds Holbeck shed at this time so could have worked a normal train to the city or perhaps has been employed on a railtour. No. 45562 was particularly in demand during 1967 and was used on six tours; the last took place in West Yorkshire during late October 1967 and the engine was condemned shortly after. Photograph by Revd J. David Benson courtesy A1 Steam Trust.

Opposite below YORK STATION

Thompson B1 no. 61093 is at York station on 3rd June 1965. Allocated to Doncaster depot at this time a transfer to Langwith Junction would occur the following month, but the engine was quickly withdrawn. Photograph by Geoff Warnes.

YORK SHED

A line of withdrawn locomotives at York shed in mid-1965. Gresley V2 no. 60847 *St Peter's School* is nearest, followed by Peppercorn A1 no. 60152 *Holyrood* and two unidentified V2s. Photograph by Roger Bastin courtesy A1 Steam Trust.

Above YORK

Thompson B1 no. 61289 entered service from the NBLC in February 1948 to Darlington shed. In January 1957 the engine transferred to Hull Botanic Gardens, then later moved to Hull Dairycoates. At York on 28th March 1966, no. 61289 was withdrawn in June 1967. Photograph by Geoff Warnes.

Below YORK SHED

A Stanier 8F with a Stanier 'Jubilee' and WD 'Austerity' – all unidentified – are at York shed on 19th March 1966. Photograph by Geoff Warnes.

Above YORK STATION
Worsdell J72 0-6-0T no. 68735 is light engine at York station in mid-1950. The engine was a long-term resident at York. Photograph by Geoffrey Oates.

Below YORK SHED
Ivatt 4MT no. 43155 is one of several locomotives in the yard at York. Photograph by Bill Reed.

Above YORK SHED

Peppercorn A1 Class no. 60155 *Borderer* is between duties at York shed on 13th September 1964. Photograph by Gerald T. Robinson.

Below YORK SOUTH SHED

Fletcher J77 Class 0-4-4T no. 68431 stands inside the derelict roundhouse known as York South shed c. 1960. Photograph by Bill Reed.

Above YORK STATION

Peppercorn A1 Pacific no. 60127 *Wilson Worsdell* is at the platform at York station with an express during August 1959. Photograph by Geoff Parrish courtesy A1 Steam Trust.

Below YORK STATION

A train of empty stock has arrived at platform eight, York station, in readiness for passengers joining the service to Liverpool on 26th May 1958; Stanier Class 5 no. 44688 is at the head. Photograph by B.W.L. Brooksbank.

Above YORK

Just south of York on 25th June 1964, Stanier Class 5 no. 44667 is passing with a train of empty bolster wagons bound for Middlesbrough's Newport Yard. Photograph by B.W.L. Brooksbank.

Below YORK STATION

At the point where the Scarborough line (right) passes over the ECML, Worsdell J71 Class 0-6-0T no. 68246 has been captured with a train of empty stock on 26th May 1958. Photograph by B.W.L. Brooksbank.

BIBLIOGRAPHY

Allen, C.J. *Titled Trains of Great Britain*. 1983.

Bradley, V.J. *Industrial Locomotives of Yorkshire Part A: The National Coal Board including Opencast Disposal Points & British Coal in West Yorkshire and North Yorkshire*. 2002.

Dow, George. *Great Central Volumes One to Three*.

Griffiths, Roger and Paul Smith. *The Directory of British Engine Sheds and Principal Locomotive Servicing Points: 2 North Midlands, Northern England and Scotland*. 2000.

Haresnape, Brian. *Fowler Locomotives*. 1997.

Haresnape, Brian. *Stanier Locomotives*. 1974.

Hawkins, Chris and George Reeve. *LMS Engine Sheds: Volume Two The Midland Railway*. 1981.

Hoole, K. *A Regional History of the Railways of Great Britain Volume 4: The North East*. 1965.

Hooper, J. *The WD Austerity 2-8-0 – The BR Record*. 2010.

Industrial Railway Society. *Industrial Railways and Locomotives of South Yorkshire – The Coal Industry 1947-1964*. 2007.

Joy, David. *A Regional History of the Railways of Great Britain Volume 8: South and West Yorkshire*. 1975.

Quick, Michael. *Railway Passenger Stations in Great Britain: A Chronology*. 2009.

RCTS. *British Railways Standard Steam Locomotives Volumes One to Four*.

RCTS. *Locomotives of the LNER Parts 1-10*.

Sixsmith, Ian. *The Book of the Ivatt Class 4 2-6-0s*. 2012.

Walmsley, Tony. *Shed by Shed Part Two: Eastern*. 2010.

Wrottesley, John. *The Great Northern Railway Volumes One to Three*.

Also available from Great Northern by Peter Tuffrey

The Last Days of Scottish Steam

The Last Years of Yorkshire Steam

The Golden Age of Yorkshire Railways

Gresley's A3s

Peppercorn's Pacifics

London Midland Steam 1948-1966

The Last Years of North East Steam

British Railways Standard Pacifics

Western Steam 1948-1966

The Last Years of North West Steam

Gresley's V2s

Southern Steam 1948-1967

visit www.*greatnorthernbooks.co.uk* for details.